Extremely WEIRD

ANIMAL HUNTERS

Text by Sarah Lovett

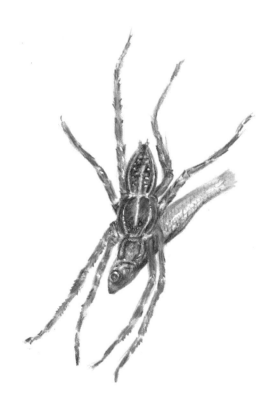

John Muir Publications
Santa Fe, New Mexico

John Muir Publications, P.O. Box 613, Santa Fe, New Mexico 87504

First edition. First printing March 1997.

Library of Congress Cataloging-in-Publication Data
Lovett, Sarah, 1953–
    Animal hunters / text by Sarah Lovett.
        p.   cm. — (Extremely weird)
    Includes index.
    Summary: Describes the physical characteristics and behavior
of such unusual predators as the green tree python, the fishing
spider, and the vampire bat.
    ISBN 1-56261-359-6
    1. Predatory animals—Juvenile literature. [1. Predatory animals.]
I. Title. II. Series: Lovett, Sarah, 1953– Extremely weird.
QL758.L68 1997
591.5'3—dc21   96-29847
                             CIP
                             AC

Extremely Weird Logo Art: Peter Aschwanden
Illustrations: Mary Sundstrom, Sally Blakemore
Design: Sally Blakemore
Typography: Copygraphics, Inc., Santa Fe, New Mexico
Printer: Burton & Mayer, Inc.

Distributed to the book trade by
Publishers Group West
Emeryville, California

Cover photo: Komodo Dragon, courtesy Animals Animals © Miriam Austerman

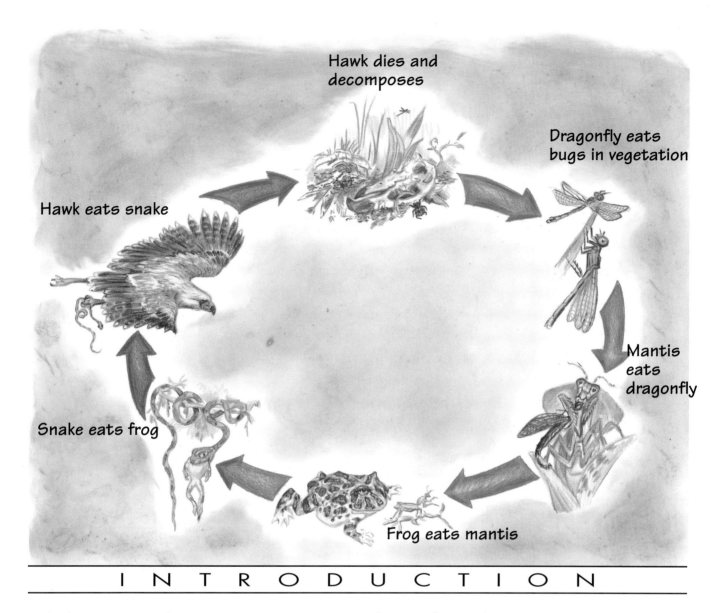

Hawk dies and decomposes

Dragonfly eats bugs in vegetation

Hawk eats snake

Mantis eats dragonfly

Snake eats frog

Frog eats mantis

INTRODUCTION

Like humans, animals must eat to survive. But animals can't shop at the grocery store when they need food like humans can. They must hunt for every bite of every meal. Animal hunters are called *predators*, and the animals they eat are called *prey*. Predators can be *carnivorous* or *omnivorous*. Carnivores only eat other animals, while omnivores, such as humans, also eat plants.

Animals may be solitary hunters, like hawks, or they may hunt in groups, like lions. Some surprise their prey through camouflage or trickery. Some use their keen senses and superior speed to overwhelm their prey. Others use their commanding strength to out-muscle their victims.

Many predators have developed unique ways to catch and eat their meals. Pythons strangle their victims. Some bats don't even use their wings to hunt—they run and hop on their feet to catch their prey. The speedy fossa of Madagascar, like a very large cat, runs faster and climbs better than other animals. Its claws are used for climbing trees and for tearing flesh. The vampire bat doesn't eat its victims—it sucks just enough blood from its prey to fill its stomach—but it's still a hunter. Other animals have long snouts which they use to burrow into holes in search of ants. Wings allow raptors, or birds of prey, to perform daring mid-flight maneuvers. A raptor's keen eyesight enables it to spot a potential meal on the ground from high in the sky before swooping down and snatching it in its sharp talons. Some hunters are not so aggressive. Animals like the mantis wait quietly for their meals to come to them.

Study the food chain diagram above to see how animals depend on each other for survival and to see how an animal can be both a predator and prey—the hunter and the hunted. Turn to the glossarized index at the back of this book if you're looking for a specific animal, or special information, or if you find a word you don't understand.

GREEN TREE PYTHON *(Chondropython viridis)*

Most people know what snakes look like; they're longish, limbless (without arms and legs), and covered with scales. What about how they sound? At most, you might hear a snake hiss, or rattle, or moan, but snakes are actually mute. Snakes have something else in common; they swallow their prey whole.

Imagine eating a whole cow whole. That would be impossible even if you wanted to try it! But some snakes can swallow a small deer whole. How can a snake get so much food into its mouth at one time? Snake jaws are specially designed for big mouthfuls. The bone that connects the lower jaw to the snake's skull works like a double-jointed hinge: the jaw drops open at the back and the front. Also, the two bones of the lower jaw stretch sideways because its chin muscles are very elastic.

Still hard to believe? Sharp teeth curving toward the snake's throat keep prey in place. Shifting its jaws side to side, bite by bite, the snake then "walks" its mouth over its victim.

Pythons and boas are giants among snakes. They kill their prey by *constriction*. Usually an animal is first caught by the snake's teeth. Then, the snake coils its body around its victim until it suffocates.

Many humans fear snakes, but only four types of constricting snakes are possibly dangerous to humans. Of those, only the South American anaconda is found in the New World. Anacondas have killed humans—but very, very rarely!

All snakes lack eyelids. Instead, their eyes are covered by skin cells. This skinny eyelid is shed when the snake molts, just like the skin on the rest of its body.

Pythons and boas are deaf, but they can "feel" loud noises with their tongues. In fact, a snake's tongue is three sense organs in one—it can touch, smell, and hear.

South American anacondas have been rumored to reach lengths of 40 feet. Reticulated pythons are reliably on record at lengths of 32.5 feet!

Charmed, I'm sure! How do snake charmers train their snakes? They don't. Snakes can't learn tricks, but they can be "handled" by humans. Snake charmers cool their snakes down before a show. A cool snake is slow and passive—and easier to handle. Unfortunately, many human "charmers" do not treat their snakes in a humane way.

ANIMAL HUNTERS

The Early Bat Gets the Bug

PALLID BAT *(Antrozous pallidus)*

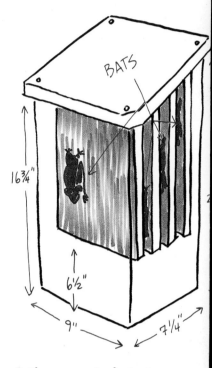

When the sun sets, the workday of the pallid bat begins—searching for juicy grasshoppers, crickets, lizards, centipedes, and even scorpions to eat. Pallid bats are "foliage gleaners," the name for all bats that capture their prey from the ground or vegetation instead of in midair. These bats probably listen for tiny footsteps with their very big ears. When they hear something good to eat, they fold their wings and hop and run on hind feet to catch their prey. These are the only bats in the habit of catching scorpions without getting harmed.

Pallid bats, from the desert Southwest, roost in dark caves, old mine shafts, and every so often, in buildings. During the summer, these pale, cream-colored creatures gather in nursery colonies of about 200 bats to raise their young. As far as we know, these bats don't migrate. Instead, they probably commute small distances and then hibernate through the winter.

Bat houses are simple structures that you can make, even if you're not a carpenter. These homes are designed to attract crevice-roosting bats to your neighborhood. Although as many as 30 bats can live in one bat house, these boxes are only a few feet square. Once complete, a bat house needs no maintenance, but be patient, it might take a year or so before bats move in.

Should you be so lucky to have a bat stop by your house for a visit, be kind to this honored guest. Open doors and windows to the outside, so the bat is able to fly away. Or, wait until it lands and approach very slowly and quietly. Gently clamp a small can or box over the bat, slide cardboard underneath, and release your visitor out of doors.

ANIMAL HUNTERS

FOSSA *(Cryptoprocta ferox)*

The fossa is a predator and the largest carnivore living in the warm, forested areas of Madagascar. Its body may grow to a length of 5 or 6 feet, and it has a sleek brown coat and a long, thin, graceful tail. Its face is marked with white eye patches topped with black triangles.

Fossas have retractile claws (like cats), and they are efficient hunters. They are also good climbers and quick runners. At night, they hunt lemurs and large birds, and their diet also includes frogs, lizards, and even insects.

The fossa lives *only* on Madagascar, the fourth largest island in the world. Madagascar is also the home of other animal species who live nowhere else. These species are very different from their relatives in other parts of the world because the island of Madagascar broke off from the mainland of Africa many millions of years ago and species evolved separately.

Because the fossa has been so heavily hunted by humans, it is listed as an endangered species. Also, most of the trees that at one time covered the island with rich, dense forests have been cut down by humans. As the forest disappears, so does the fossa and other endangered animals.

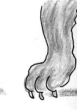

Although sometimes placed in the cat family, fossas walk on the soles of their feet like bears instead of walking on their toes like cats.

You can help: Trees need friends! To help keep the planet green: recycle paper; plant seedlings; join Tree Amigos. (*Amigos* means "friends" in Spanish.) Write: Center for Environmental Study, Tree Amigos Project, 143 Bostwick NE, Grand Rapids, MI 49503. Through Tree Amigos, you can adopt an acre of tropical rain forest or learn about other ways to help!

Introducing new species is a real threat for local wildlife. For instance, your own furry kitty cat is a deadly hunter of birds, lizards, frogs, and other wild animals. And the dingo, a wild dog, introduced to Australia by Aborigines, has helped drive native species to extinction.

ANIMAL HUNTERS

FISHING SPIDER

Big-eyed fishing spiders are pond-skaters, able to skim over the water's surface because their bodies are extremely light compared to their size. Tiny hairs, sticky and plentiful on their legs, also help provide buoyancy and traction when skating. Because they are balloon light, fishing spiders can't dive or stay underwater unless they attach themselves to leaves. Like many spiders, fishing spiders can use an air bubble for underwater breathing—but only for a very short time.

True to their name, sharp-eyed fishing spiders are known to catch very small minnows and tadpoles for dinner. Their system is to perch their two back legs on a small stone, rock, or twig and cast their other six legs out over the water. When a tadpole cruises by, the fishing spider plunges suddenly underwater and wraps its legs around the startled prey. After a great struggle, the tadpole is lugged back onto the perch and devoured.

Spiders live in almost every nook and cranny of the world, below ground and above. Indeed, spiders have been found above altitudes of 20,000 feet on Mount Everest.

ANIMAL HUNTERS

KOMODO DRAGON (*Varanus komodoensis*)

Reaching a length of 10 feet and a weight of 250 pounds, thickly armored and ancient-looking Komodo dragons are one of the the world's largest lizards.

Although Komodo bodies are big, their territory is small. In the wild, they can only be found on Komodo and a few other small islands in Indonesia.

Komodo dragons are flesh eaters. They prey on small wild deer, pigs, and domestic animals. They also work as nature's scavengers, eating the remains of dead animals.

Like all monitor lizards, Komodos have long necks, heavy bodies, and thick tails. They are also equipped with dangerous-looking claws. They use these sharp claws and their equally sharp teeth for tearing their prey into bite-sized chunks. Using a little imagination, Komodos really do look like magnificent dragons.

What's your "habitat"? Since habitat is the place you naturally live, yours might be New York, Detroit, or Amarillo. Komodo dragons have a very limited habitat of a few islands in Indonesia; unlike you, they do not survive anywhere else.

Komodo dragons are big, but another lizard, Salvador's monitor (*Varanus salvadori*), is biggest, reaching lengths of more than 18 feet!

ANIMAL HUNTERS

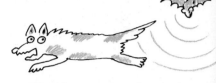

VAMPIRE BAT *(Desmodus rotundus)*

With the setting sun, Count Dracula rose from his coffin and went in search of fresh blood, sometimes taking the form of a bat—or so the story goes. For centuries, people have made up scare-raising tales about bats just for the fright of it. Actually, most bats are gentle, friendly creatures that definitely don't want to hide in your hairdo or suck your blood.

There are only three known species of vampire bats in the entire world which live on fresh blood. These are found in Mexico and parts of Central and South America. While they might be dangerous to a South American cow, they hardly ever bite humans.

At dusk, the vampire bat leaves its roost and skims low and silent over the ground in search of sleeping cattle, sheep, and horses. Landing near its victim, the bat creeps quietly forward, ready to strike. It bites with razor sharp teeth, choosing a part of the body that has no fur. This is done so painlessly, the victim doesn't even wake up. Curling its tongue like a straw, the bat laps up blood, just as a cat laps up milk. Vampire bat saliva contains anticoagulants— this can keep blood flowing for several hours—and they may feast for thirty minutes. Sometimes their stomachs are so filled with blood, they can hardly fly.

The good news is, vampire bats don't drink enough blood to harm their victims—only about one ounce. The bad news is, vampire bats sometimes carry rabies and other diseases that infect their prey. Although other kinds of bats almost never carry rabies, to avoid any problems, people should never handle them.

Although vampire bats often attack domestic animals, they hardly ever bite dogs. That's because dogs hear high-frequency sounds and know when bats are flying near.

In spite of their hair-raising reputation, vampire bats are among the few mammals that will aid each other and also care for orphaned baby bats.

The same enzymes in vampire bat saliva that keep a victim's blood flowing may soon be used to fight heart disease in humans. Scientists believe those anticoagulants will effectively dissolve human blood clots, the major cause of heart attacks.

BURP

ZZZ

ANIMAL HUNTERS

LONG-BEAKED ECHIDNA (*Zaglossus spp.*)

Spiny anteaters like the long-beaked echidna are prickly critters. Their spines are very large, specialized hairs with hollow, sharp tips which spiny anteaters use to discourage predators: they roll up into a prickly ball when threatened. Another way these anteaters avoid predators (including humans) is by wedging their bodies between rocks and in crevices. Once wedged, the anteater is just about impossible to budge!

Spiny anteaters have claws and are swift diggers capable of burrowing straight down in hard earth in search of prey. Their long snouts are used as tools to break up hollow logs and sort through leaf piles. Their lengthy tongues are covered with mucous that sticks to their favorite foods—termites, insects, and worms. Since spiny anteaters have no teeth, they use the horny ridges on the back of their tongue to grind up each mouthful.

These anteaters are unusual animals when it comes to reproduction. Unlike most mammals, they do not give birth to live young. Instead, during the breeding season, the female's belly gets a pouch or pocket. After mating with the male, the female lays a single leathery egg that is placed inside the pouch to incubate for less than two weeks. The baby anteater breaks out of the shell with the help of an eggtooth.

The long-beaked echidna, from the humid forests of New Guinea, is one of several anteater species listed as endangered. It has been overhunted by humans who eat its flesh.

You can help: A few years ago, kids in Sweden heard about rain forests in trouble. They sold T-shirts, worked odd jobs, and asked for donations. The money they raised was sent to scientists who bought 15 acres of rain forest. When kids all over the world heard about the forest, they raised money, too. More than 14,000 acres have been saved so far. The Children's Rain Forest is a nature preserve where everything—birds, monkeys, frogs, lizards, beetles, and trees—is protected! It's a rain forest your own kids can visit in the future.

The biblical story of Noah's ark was one of the first mentions of humans taking responsibility for saving animals from extinction. Noah wanted three pairs of each species. Unfortunately, that's not enough to ensure survival.

ANIMAL HUNTERS

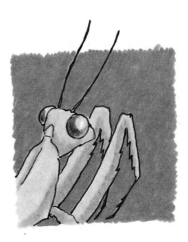

CRYPTIC MANTIS (*Choeradolis sp.*)

Mantis is Greek for "soothsayer" or "prophet," and it is the name given this insect group by Swedish naturalist Carolus Linnaeus who lived in the eighteenth century. Although mantids look very wise and saintly, they are fierce predators who use their "praying arms" to lash out and impale their victims. Mantids depend on excellent eyesight to spot prey, and they are able to attack with great speed. They feed on insects (often other mantids) and other invertebrates as well as frogs, lizards, and small birds. Mantids don't go in search of prey. Instead, they lie in ambush.

Most of the 1,800 mantid species depend on camouflage to surprise their victims. Because their wings are patterned with leaflike designs and their limbs are long and twiglike, they are able to blend in with their background. Some even mimic bark and tree moss. Depending on the species, mantids come in a variety of lengths, from one to five inches.

Mantids are very easy to recognize because they have a movable head, a slender body, and prehensile legs (the better to grasp their prey). They lay their eggs in foamy, papery egg capsules. Each capsule may contain 200 eggs, and a female might produce as many as five capsules each year. Although the eggs are deposited in the fall, they do not hatch until the following spring. The cryptic mantis (and most mantids) prefers warm or tropical climates.

Praying mantises are named for their posture at rest; their front legs are folded and zipped together by interlocking spines into a "praying" position.

In African folklore, mantids are sometimes used to represent spirits and gods.

Mantids and cockroaches are related, but cockroaches are nocturnal (active at night) herbivores while mantids are diurnal (active in the day) predators.

Photo, facing page, courtesy Animals Animals © G. I. Bernard

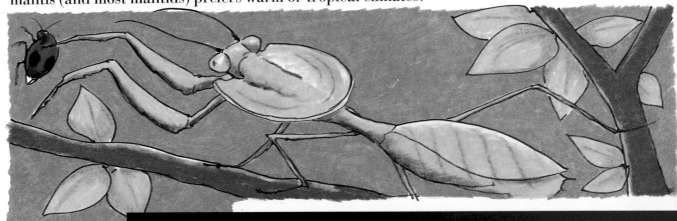

ANIMAL HUNTERS

SOUTH AMERICAN HORNED FROG (*Ceratophrys ornata*)

MARY SUNDSTROM

The South American horned frog has a powerful jaw and sharp, toothlike fangs— the better to eat small mammals, snakes, birds, turtles, and other frogs. This frog likes to sit and wait for prey to pass by. Its colorful, armored skin provides great camouflage among leaves, dirt, and grasses where it burrows so deeply that only its bulging eyes are visible.

Most relatives of the South American horned frog are odd-looking. Many have body armor—thick shields of dense skin covering their back and head—that makes them too much of a mouthful for predators to swallow. Some species grow to eight inches long and almost as wide; others are tiny, barely one inch long when fully grown.

When the rainy season ends, the South American horned frog is one of a group of species that burrow into the ground and form cocoons to encase their bodies. The cocoon is like parchment and is made of layers of dried skin and mucous secretions. It encases the entire frog except for two air vents at the nostrils. Once in their cocoons, frogs can live for many months (maybe even years), and then . . . just add water!

Waterproof! Frogs are amphibians, which means they are "creatures that live in both places"—in water and on land. Frogs need water to mate, lay eggs, raise tadpoles, and just to survive. In order to conserve water, frogs have developed surprising ways to "waterproof" themselves in dry seasons. Waterproofing keeps the water in, not out. Some frogs form cocoons and stay encased for months; others ooze a waxy mucous that shields them during the day when they're not very active.

ANIMAL HUNTERS

BLUNT-HEADED TREE SNAKE (*Imantodes cenchoa*)

No doubt about it, blunt-headed tree snakes are weird looking: they have an extremely slim body, a big head, and big eyes. They also do weird things—such as act like an I-beam girder to bridge the gaps between branches where they hang out. Blunt-headed tree snakes will change their shape slightly and stiffen their body to reach a distant branch. Once they firmly attach to the new branch, their body relaxes again.

Blunt-headed tree snakes become active at dusk, and they hunt—for anoles, geckos, and other lizards—during the night. In daylight, they prefer to coil and rest in leaf clumps or in the leaf whorls of bromeliad plants. Several blunt-headed tree snakes may share the same resting place.

Blunt-headed tree snake habitat extends from the forests of southern Mexico to Bolivia and Paraguay. They hatch from eggs, and adults may reach a length of more than 100 centimeters (over 3 feet).

More than 250 million years ago, reptiles first crept out of the shallow seas and ventured on land. The evolutionary effort was worth it; on land, there were plenty of insects to eat and dense forests for shelter. Today, lizards, turtles, snakes, crocodilians, and the rare tuatara are the five groups of reptiles found on earth.

Blunt-headed tree snakes have fangs in the rear of their mouth. They strike their prey swiftly and accurately.

ANIMAL HUNTERS

HAIRY MYGALOMORPH

Tarantulas are primitive spiders, which means they look a lot like their ancient ancestors. Around 360 million years ago, tarantula-like spiders crawled through swampy, steamy forests—the same forests that became today's coal supply for North America and Europe.

Because their fangs point "backward" under their body, tarantulas must throw themselves back and up to drive their fangs into prey. Although they strike with speed, getting ready can be a clumsy operation. More modern true spiders have fangs that are "cross-eyed." They can strike more efficiently without lifting their bodies up.

Legs are organs of touch for spiders, especially important for tarantulas because their eyesight is poor. They rely on touch—using their front legs and pedipalps—to find and capture prey. All spiders do have the ability to tell what tastes bad, sowbugs and stinkbugs, for instance, but not in the same way humans do. And while we have hairs in our nose and ears that help us smell and hear, spiders have hairs containing chemical receptors covering the *outside* of their bodies.

Some mygalomorphs are trap-door spiders—nifty critters that use the spines on their chelicerae as diggers to tunnel out bits of earth from their underground burrows. The earth is rolled into balls and carefully removed until the tunnel is complete. But these spiders are especially famous for their trap-doors—little hinged lids that fit tight to keep out rain and unwanted visitors. Braced against the walls of their tunnels, trap-door spiders can hold the door so tightly shut that not even an arachnologist can force it open.

YUK STINK BUG!

ANIMAL HUNTERS

DEWEY GREEN DARNER *(Anax junius)*

Darners are large, brightly colored dragonflies. Like all members of their family, they have a stout body, a large, movable head, and two pairs of large veiny wings. They also boast huge compound eyes (some can see in almost all directions at once, the better to spot their prey) and have biting and chewing mouthparts.

Dragonflies are fierce predators, and they pursue their prey—mosquitoes, flies, and gnats—on the wing. In flight, their bristly legs are used to clutch their victims while their long wings keep them airborne.

Dragonflies usually prefer habitats close to streams, lakes, and other permanent water sources. They need fresh water, in which their eggs hatch and the young reach maturity.

Dragonfly eggs are deposited in jellied masses that stick to water plants for several days. The newly hatched dragonfly nymph has no wings, and it may not mature for two or three years. During this immature stage of its life cycle, it lives completely underwater feeding on small fishes and tadpoles. When it grows large enough, the nymph crawls out of the water and molts to emerge as a fully winged dragonfly.

Darner species range from Alaska to Hawaii and the eastern coast of Asia. They are swift and graceful flyers whose wings are glassy; their abdomen is brilliant blue, and their brow is emerald green. Unlike most other dragonfies, adult darners can live far from water.

Skimmers are big colorful dragonflies often seen skimming shallow water or "sitting guard" on plants. They protect their territory from other dragonflies.

MMMMMM! Darners got their name because they were said to sew a child's mouth closed. But that's just a folktale!

To breathe underwater, the dewey green darner nymph uses internal gills that are in the form of ridges of tissue in its rectum. The nymph draws in and expels water across the ridges. If water is expelled very quickly, the nymph is jet propelled!

Photo, facing page, courtesy Animals Animals © John Gerlach

ANIMAL HUNTERS

GENET (Genetta genetta)

Deep in a rocky burrow in the forests and on the grasslands and plains of Europe and Africa, the genet sleeps away its day. At night, in contrast, this small meat-eater (carnivore) might climb trees to hunt for nesting and roosting birds, although most of its prey is captured on the ground. The genet seems to glide over the earth. That's because it walks on its digits in what has been described as a "waltzing trot."

Genets usually travel alone or in pairs. They communicate with each other using a variety of vocal and visual signals. They also have a keen sense of smell. Like skunks, genets can send smelly messages from the anal scent glands located on their rear ends.

You might think of the genet as a distant relative of the mongoose, although some scientists believe the mongoose belongs to its very own family. Both have short legs, a pointy snout, and a long tail, but the genet looks more like a cat than the mongoose does.

If a genet can fit its head through an opening, its body can always follow. That's because its body is slender and loosely jointed.

Genets have retractable claws—they extend and recede—the better to catch frogs, lizards, rodents, insects, spiders, and even fruit, bulbs, and nuts. Some genets eat carrion.

Photo, facing page, courtesy Animals Animals © Michael Dick

ANIMAL HUNTERS

Eagle Eye

HARPY EAGLE (Harpia harpyja)

Hawks, vultures, falcons, and ospreys are all diurnal birds of prey—raptors that are active during the day. So are eagles. There are more than 200 species of these meat-eaters occupying most of the world except for Antarctica and Oceania.

Raptors come in a variety of sizes— from the pygmy falcon (about the size of a smallish dove) to the huge Andean condor, which has a 10-foot wingspan. Most raptors have a bill that is a sharp hook and feet that are powerful and equipped with razor-edged talons. Females are often larger than their mates, and usually both sexes share in the duties of nest-building, egg incubation, feeding, and protection of the young.

The harpy eagle from South America may qualify as one of the world's strongest birds of prey. The harpy lives on the edges of rain forests and hunts capuchin, squirrel, and woolly monkeys as well as sloths and tree porcupines, which it tears from the branches using its talons. Harpy eagles have even been known to kill small dogs and baby pigs.

They are solitary hunters, and males and females pair up only during courtship. Harpies line their treetop nests with leaves, ferns, moss, and the bones of their prey. Males are allowed in nest territory only long enough to drop off food for the female and her young.

Native people have long valued the harpy eagle's feathers. The shiny white, gray, and black plumes are exchanged for food and other items.

Hawks and eagles are famed for their keen eyesight. Their retinas are chock-full of visual cells— eight times as many as people have. High-flying at 10,000 feet above ground, we humans could just make out a pronghorn antelope if we looked very closely. At the same distance, most birds of prey would see it clearly, at a glance.

Eagles, hawks, and other birds of prey swoop down on their prey and use their long talons to tear or strike.

Peregrine falcons, the world's speediest birds, have been clocked pursuing prey in dives of 175 miles per hour! They slash their victims with razor-sharp claws and force them to the ground.

ANIMAL HUNTERS

This glossarized index will help you find specific information on animals and animal hunters. It will also help you understand the meaning of some of the words used in this book.